IMAGES
of America

AROUND
CAYUGA
COUNTY

The *Dorothy* at Casowasco, early twentieth century. This two-story, rustic-design building was the central dock at Casowasco, the Case family summerhouse on Owasco Lake. In addition to the central dock, the estate included northern and southern boathouses. The *Dorothy* was a large, steam-powered vessel that was eventually lost to fire. The Case family represents many generations of local investors. Theodore Case, together with E.I. Sponable, invented the first commercially successful system of recording sound film at the Case Research Lab in Auburn. Casowasco is now a conference center that can be rented for meetings, and many of the estate's original buildings are still in use. The Case Research Lab, located behind the Cayuga Museum, is open to the public as a restored historic site.

IMAGES
of America

AROUND
CAYUGA
COUNTY

Stephanie E. Przybylek and Peter Lloyd Jones

ARCADIA

First published 1996
Copyright © Stephanie E. Przybylek and Peter Lloyd Jones, 1996

ISBN 0-7524-0431-8

Published by Arcadia Publishing,
an imprint of the Chalford Publishing Corporation
One Washington Center, Dover, New Hampshire 03820
Printed in Great Britain

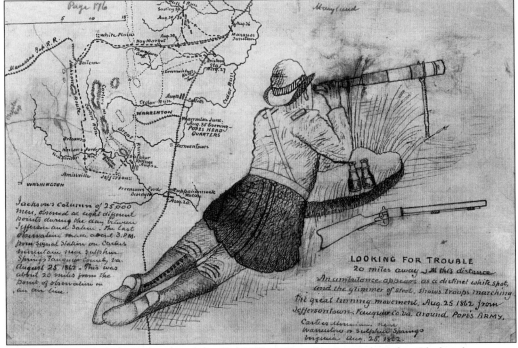

Colonel John Clark, participant in the Civil War. This drawing is by John Clark, who was an aide-de-camp to General Banks during the Civil War and a lifelong resident of Cayuga County. Scouting the enemy, Clark recorded the movements of the Confederate Army on their march to Manassas, prior to the Second Battle of Bull Run. He gave this information to General Pope, who could have acted on it and prepared the Union Army for attack, but no action was taken and the moment was lost. Nevertheless, Clark understood the import of his deed and drew this map, with himself shown witnessing the troop movements, for his private collections. Clark's Civil War maps, Native American research, and personal papers are in the collections of the Cayuga Museum.

Contents

Sales meeting of the International Time Recording Company, c. 1900. The two brothers identified as Bundys are the founders of Bundy Time Recording Co., which evolved into I.T.R. and later, IBM. Willard invented the time clock, and Harlow built an industry and created a brilliant marketing plan to sell this new invention to the world. Harlow was born in Auburn, where the brothers were raised; he attended Hamilton College and settled for a time in Oneonta. Willard remained in Auburn, operating his jewelry store until the two of them removed to Binghamton to manufacture the time clock. Willard's monumental clock, together with examples of time clocks and the early history of IBM, are on display at the Cayuga Museum.

Introduction

This, the second photographic history in the Images of America series by the staff of the Cayuga Museum, differs from the first in that its primary consideration is the towns and villages outside of Auburn. Additionally, while the first book, *Around Auburn*, included images only from the collections of the Cayuga Museum, this book relies primarily on the collections of local historical societies and individuals.

While researching this book, it soon became apparent that although county borders offer a meaningful political division of a region, they do not present a meaningful division of culture and commerce, nor do they define or influence a community's sense of place. Incorporated in 1799, the county originally included the northern portion of what is now Tompkins County, all of Seneca County, and part of Wayne County. In 1817, the county's borders were redrawn to the area that they now define, ending just south of King Ferry. The present western boundary runs through Cayuga Lake and north from that point. The borders of Cayuga County outline a narrow strip of land whose width varies from between 5.5 and 21 miles, while its length measures at over 54 miles. The communities at its northern and southern extremes interact today barely more than they did two hundred years ago, when travel from one end to the other took more than a day.

This book leaves with its reader an overall impression of the deeply rural character of this county. Auburn, although it is the county's central city, is still a small city. Many of the inhabitants throughout the county often travel to towns and cities in the surrounding counties for commerce and culture.

The economic and cultural character of Cayuga County has been influenced by the land itself, whose morphology was defined by the many glaciers that moved through this region. These glaciers carved the deep north-south valleys that became the Finger Lakes, deposited the drumlin fields, and created the steep hills with hanging valleys that, through thousands of years of erosion, developed into many dramatic waterfalls. The work of glaciers has provided the county with rich soil for farming, lakes for sport and commerce, and hills and waterfalls for beauty.

Cayuga County takes its name from one of the five original nations of the Iroquois Federation. The Cayuga people occupied the region west of the Onondaga and east of the Seneca, including all of Cayuga County and much of Seneca and Tompkins Counties. To the Iroquois, the Cayuga were known as the People of the Marsh. The Cayuga people lived freely in this region until their land was devastated by General Sullivan and his men during the Revolutionary War.

Sullivan's campaign to punish the Cayuga was justified by the fact that the Cayuga had sided with the British and participated with Butler's Rangers in depredations on the New York frontier. As a result of the campaign against them, there were few Cayuga people left following the Revolutionary War, and when their reservation was later established, only a handful remained to occupy the land.

Following the Revolutionary War, many veterans acquired military tracts in this county. A few of the veterans subsequently moved to the area, but many used their claim as an investment, selling their shares off quickly at inflated prices. Those that did settle the area cleared the land for farming and established an agricultural economy that exists to this day.

This book is divided into eight chapters, each concerned with a specific area of the county. The common themes throughout these chapters are: farming, villages, and water. Throughout the rise and fall of the county's manufacturing industry, which was located primarily in Auburn, the farms, the villages, and—of course—the water, remained. In this way, it is the enduring rural communities that offer the primary character of this county.

Many of the farms in this county have been handed down through generations, while others have changed hands to new, unknown owners. While the opening of the Midwest caused most New England farms to be abandoned, the richness of the land in this county has allowed farming to remain as an important industry. Many of the photographs in this book tell the stories of individual struggles on these farms and in the small communities—stories of lives dedicated to family, and to community.

The many villages dotting the countryside throughout this county have been able to maintain most of their original charm and character. Many of these villages also still have a general store that serves as both marketplace and meeting place for their community. In many cases, these stores operate out of the same nineteenth-century buildings in which they were originally founded. It is our hope that this book will help inspire the reader to take the time to drive around the county and visit these villages, to see the sites included in these photographs.

The lakes within this county have long provided beauty, recreation, and a path for commerce. As can be seen from the images in this book, many steamers plied the lakes in the nineteenth century, both to transport people from town to town, and to serve as simply a great way to spend an afternoon. The lakes also acted as a catalyst for the construction of hotels, restaurants, parks, homes, and villages. However, these places never became too large, because the lakes also limited the growth of mass transportation. For most residents of this county, it is unbelievable that some states do not have a single natural lake within their borders. To live without our lakes would be impossible. This is not just a county of lakes, it is a county of people of the lakes.

In completing this photographic history of Cayuga County, the authors wish to express their appreciation to the following institutions, organizations, and individuals, without whose support this project would not have been possible: Roy Bench; Tom Eldred, county historian, and Malcom Goodelle, county archivist, the Cayuga County Historian's Office; the Civic Heritage Historical Society; Lou and Myrtle Chomyk; Susan Robey, curator, the DeWitt Historical Society of Tompkins County; the Frontenanc Historical Society; the Genoa Historical Association; Mrs. and Mrs. Ed Kabelac; the Lock 52 Historical Society of Port Byron; Helen Bergamo, archivist,the Louis J. Long Library, Wells College; Dorothy Southard, town of Ira historian; the late Evelyn Wood, town of Victory historian; Joni Lincoln, town of Conquest historian; Marion Dudley, village of Meridian and town of Cato historian; and Don Richardson, the Sterling Historical Association.

We hope our readers enjoy this short pictorial journey through time and around Cayuga County as much as we enjoyed assembling this collection.

One
Auburn

Lehigh Valley Railroad Depot, State Street, Auburn, c. 1900. This north-south rail line, which ran along Owasco Lake, began as the Southern Central Railroad in the 1860s. It functioned as a means of linking the Great Lakes to the Southern Tier. In the 1880s, it was taken over by the Lehigh and New York Railroad Company, which then leased the line to the Lehigh Valley Railroad.

Side porch of Seward House, William Seward and family, late nineteenth century. Seward, secretary of state to President Lincoln, is seated to the far right.

Seward House, late nineteenth century. This is a view from the side porch, looking out on the gardens, with William Seward sitting in the chair.

Auburn Theological Seminary grounds, early twentieth century. This view includes Morgan Hall, Willard Chapel, and the Dodge-Morgan library. Founded in 1818 by Presbyterians, the Auburn Theological Seminary was an important factor in Auburn's religious and cultural life until it closed its Auburn doors in 1939.

Interior, shoe-cutting shop of Dunn & McCarthy, 1920s. In 1867 Dunn, Salmon and Company was organized to market shoes manufactured in the Auburn State Prison. Founder John Dunn Jr. hired Charles McCarthy in 1876 to increase promotion of his product. By 1889, the company, then known as Dunn & McCarthy, was located in the factory complex of the old Josiah Barber woolen mill on Washington Street. Dunn & McCarthy was incorporated in 1896, and that same year F.L. Emerson joined the firm. Emerson, who became president upon the retirement of McCarthy, was the first person to adapt assembly-line methods to the shoe industry. Dunn & McCarthy also became one of the first shoe companies to offer products in standard sizes and widths.

D.M. Osborne & Co. exhibit, Palace of Agriculture, St. Louis World's Fair, 1904. The Osborne Company touted this display of agricultural products as being the "only exhibit in which both grain and grass machines are kept in motion."

Workers from D.M. Osborne & Co. Malleable Iron Works and Rolling Mills, late nineteenth or early twentieth century. The factory, which was located on Pulsifer Street, was on the line of the New York Central & Hudson River Railroad.

Derailed flat car, *c.* 1900. Shown on the rail line beside the Dunn & McCarthy factory complex, this car was carrying New Birdsall Company agricultural equipment.

Schicht System Shop, Office Supplies and Printing, *c.* 1915. This office supply company, which advertised itself as "The Business Man's Department Store," was located at 21 Dill Street, and later at 34–36 State Street.

Scotch Woolen Co., *c.* 1904. This clothing store is only listed in the City Directories as being located at 86 Genesee Street, but apparently its owners had a peculiar infatuation with the number 145.

Cuddy & Geherin Coal Company, Genesee Street office. Started in 1909, Cuddy & Geherin had their offices at 19 1/2 Genesee Street and their yard at 73 Clark Street. The large piece of anthracite coal in the window was given to Cuddy & Geherin in 1934, in honor of the 25th anniversary of their business It was presented by the Lehigh Navigation Coal Company, one of the mining establishments in the anthracite region of Pennsylvania. Charles Geherin donated the anthracite to the Cayuga Museum.

C.B. Quick's Grocery, corner of Orchard and Washington Streets, *c.* 1889. Note the street signs attached to the side of the building. Although the demographics of the neighborhood have changed, a community store still exists on this site, as does the apartment building in the background.

Interior of the restaurant at the Garrett Hotel, later the Woodlock Hotel, on the corner of State and Water Streets, *c.* 1920s.

Auburn Diner, front entrance, 1930s. This diner is located on the site of the old New York Central Railroad depot. The painted signs on the building's exterior advertise a standard diner tradition—customary all-night service. Bixler was the name of the diner car manufacturer. The Auburn State Prison can be seen in the background.

Auburn Diner, Timothy Flood proprietor, 1930s. The diner was brought to this location by rail, and, although recently damaged by fire, it is still located at 120 State Street across from the Auburn Prison.

Old South Street parking lot. The building at the far right was the location of the Colby Radio Company, one of the earliest manufacturers of radios in the country. It later became a supply and repair company for all brands of radios.

Unidentified child on Auburn porch front, early twentieth century. The boy's props and outfit surely suggest the celebration of a patriotic holiday. The ship model is the *Kankakee*, which resembles the type of battleship used during the Spanish-American War. The boy's hat has "Maine" embroidered on it, recalling that famous ship.

Two
Owasco Lake and Points South

The steamer *City of Auburn*, early twentieth century. Packed with summer guests, the boat is heading through the Owasco Outlet toward Owasco Lake. In the nineteenth century, steamers such as this were used for transportation to sites around Owasco Lake. The *City of Auburn* and the *Lady of the Lake* were two of the more well known of these boats.

Baseball game in progress, c. 1916. This photograph was taken by Charles J. Heiser from the highest point of the old Figure-Eight Roller Coaster at Lakeside Park.

Figure-Eight Roller Coaster, Island Park, early twentieth century. At the time of the photograph, water had been drained for work on the seawall. Island Park was named for the island created by the dredging of the Owasco Outlet in the 1880s. The area became a popular picnic site for boaters, and developed into an amusement center by the end of the nineteenth century.

Seaplane and amusement pavilion, Lakeside Park, 1920s. Both the old Figure Eight and Owasco Dips Roller Coasters are visible in the background. Lakeside Park offered rides, sporting events, concerts, dances, and water sports, just to name a few of the popular activities available. Prior to World War II, the park was a big attraction throughout the central New York region. The seaplane ride in the foreground gave everybody the opportunity to pilot their own plane.

A seaplane landing in the Owasco Outlet, Lakeside Park, 1920s. Although this plane looks as if it might have been thrown from the seaplane ride, it is an actual seaplane visiting Lakeside Park. The large turn of the Wasco Dips Roller Coaster and the tunnel of the Mill Chute Ride are visible in the background.

Upper house at Willowbrook, late nineteenth century. This house was part of the sprawling Throop-Martin estate which stood along the northeast shores of Owasco Lake. The site was a popular destination for generals and other dignitaries throughout the 1800s because of the estate's beauty and its hosts' grace. As later generations of the Martin family moved on to other regions to pursue other dreams, the house was abandoned. It was razed in 1960, and all that remains of the site is the willow, the brook, and a state historical marker.

Myles Keogh and Andrew Alexander, 1860s. General Alexander married Evy Martin of Willowbrook, and introduced Keogh to her sister Nelly. Some believe that Nelly harbored an unrequited love for Keogh, who was killed at the Battle of Little Bighorn with Colonel Custer in 1876. Keogh wrote Nelly prior to his death, asking to be buried in the Willowbrook area if he did not return from that campaign. Nelly honored this request, and Keogh was reinterred in the Martin family plot in Fort Hill Cemetery.

Billy Claxton, the "Hermit of Owasco Lake," early twentieth century. Claxton is shown sitting in front of his Ocean House at Conklin's Point. He sold essentials such as candy and birch beer from his small store, catering to summer picnic guests at Conklin's Point.

John D. Rockefeller's boyhood home, Rockefeller Road. This modest home is where John D. Rockefeller lived for a few years as a small boy. His father, William, is the subject of the book *Joshua of the Finger Lakes* by Charles Brutcher, in which he is depicted as a horse thief. It is said that the Rockefeller family tried to buy all existing copies of the book, and denied ever having lived in this area. (Morton photograph, courtesy DeWitt Historical Society of Tompkins County.)

Lady of the Lake in dry dock, late nineteenth century. The photograph shows an unidentified location along Owasco Lake. (Courtesy Roy Bench.)

Cascade Hotel, Cascade-On-Owasco. This hotel, located on the southwest corner of Owasco Lake, was one of many popular vacation resorts on Owasco Lake in the nineteenth century. This view from above the rail line was taken by Vern Morton, who was a professional photographer from nearby Groton in Tompkins County. (Morton photograph, courtesy DeWitt Historical Society of Tompkins County.)

Boardwalk and shaded paths, Cascade-On-Owasco. Morton photographed many of the waterfalls in the south-central Finger Lakes region, showing his fascination with this beautiful natural phenomenon. (Morton photograph, courtesy DeWitt Historical Society of Tompkins County.)

Waterfall at Cascade. (Morton photograph, courtesy DeWitt Historical Society of Tompkins County.)

Lower waterfall at Cascade. A dog, a man, and fish, some of whom will enjoy this particular summer afternoon more than others. (Morton photograph, courtesy DeWitt Historical Society of Tompkins County.)

Summer cabin at Cascade-on-Owasco, Owasco Lake. This picture is a good example of the difference in architecture between a summer cottage and a year-round residence at the turn of the century. (Morton photograph, courtesy DeWitt Historical Society of Tompkins County.)

Spirit of St. Louis, the private airport on Rockefeller Road, late 1920s. After Lindbergh's triumphant solo flight across the Atlantic Ocean, he toured America, stopping at hundreds of airports around the county to meet each local community. His stop in Cayuga County was at a small airport high on a hill above Koenig's Point, on the east shore of Owasco Lake. (Courtesy Roy Bench.)

Crowd greeting the landing of the *Spirit of St. Louis*, late 1920s. Charles Lindbergh is the small figure standing above the others in the center background.

Lehigh Valley Depot, early twentieth century, Moravia. Moravia is located on the southern end of Owasco Lake. This north-south rail line traveled up the west side of Owasco Lake on its way from Moravia to Auburn. For many years, homes on the west side of the lake were only accessible by boat or by this train.

Moravia House, early twentieth century, Moravia. This hostelry was built in 1820 and was a famed gathering place for local horsemen. The building was razed in 1929, after witnessing over one hundred years of service to the community.

View along Main Street, Moravia, early twentieth century. Notice the very unique tower clock on the right with a face as tall as a man. This clock was located on Fireman's Hall. It is doubtful that anyone in Moravia needed a watch.

Smith's Hall, Main Street, late nineteenth century, Moravia.

Fireman's Hall with clock tower, Moravia, early twentieth century. Notice the bell tower on the building's rear. The location of the clock today remains a mystery.

Parade along Main Street, Moravia, late nineteenth or early twentieth century.

Cow Shed, Fillmore Glen, Moravia. Pictures such as this one allow for the study of erosion in the glen during the last one hundred years. (Morton photograph, courtesy DeWitt Historical Society of Tompkins County.)

Stone bridge, foot of Fillmore Glen, Moravia. This glen was named for President Millard Fillmore, who was born and raised in the southern part of Cayuga County. A replica of his home now stands in Fillmore Glen on the flat below the falls. (Morton photograph, courtesy DeWitt Historical Society of Tompkins County.)

Carpenter Falls, located east of New Hope. These falls, with their dramatic shelf and amphitheater, stand above the western shore of Skaneateles Lake. The site has long been a popular summer attraction, but it has never been developed into a public park. (Morton photograph, courtesy DeWitt Historical Society of Tompkins County.)

Cemetery footbridge across Montville Creek, Moravia, late nineteenth century. This unusual bridge was located east of Moravia. Its rusted sides are all that remain, and even the trail is indistinguishable from the overgrown woods that surround the site.

Locke Lehigh Valley Depot. The village of Locke was the first stop on the rail line south of Moravia. This small community sits in the Owasco Valley to the west of Summer Hill. (Morton photograph, courtesy DeWitt Historical Society of Tompkins County.)

Odd Fellows Hall and Main Street, Locke, early twentieth century. (Morton photograph, courtesy DeWitt Historical Society of Tompkins County.)

New church bell for the Locke Methodist Church. (Morton photograph, courtesy DeWitt Historical Society of Tompkins County.)

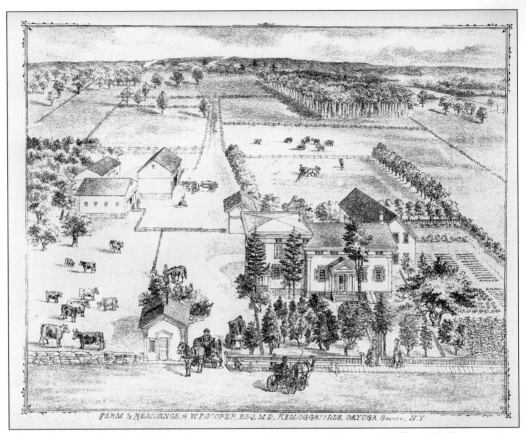

FARM & RESIDENCE of W.F.COOPER, ESQ, M.D. KELLOGGSVILLE, CAYUGA County, N.Y

Home of Dr. William Cooper, cousin to James Fennimore Cooper. William F. Cooper was a medical doctor who lived in Kelloggsville, located just west of New Hope on the ridge above Skaneateles Lake. Dr. Cooper was a powerful leader of his community. In the book *Joshua of the Finger Lakes*, he appears as one of the few men who stood up against William Rockefeller. The Cayuga Museum owns several of Cooper's belongings, including a detective's journal of a very interesting murder that Cooper helped investigate.

Three

Along Cayuga Lake: Cayuga and Union Springs

Mansfield Block, with a view of Mansfield House, village of Cayuga, late nineteenth or early twentieth century. The village of Cayuga was once a major crossroads, including the port of the Cayuga-Seneca Canal, a railroad station, and the Cayuga Bridge, which offered the most direct route to the west across the northern end of Cayuga Lake. Today the bridge is gone, and the train no longer stops, but the village has maintained its scenic appeal, located high on a bluff above the lake. With the recent addition of a deep-water marina, Cayuga's economy is turning to tourism.

Boater near the Little Cayuga Canal drawbridge for the New York Central & Hudson railroad through Cayuga, late nineteenth century. The American Malting Company malt house and evaporator are visible in the background. In 1926, the Beacon Milling Company purchased this vacant property for the production of animal feeds. Beacon Milling became one of the leaders of the commercial feed industry, and was one of the first companies to consider scientific nutritional research as an essential element of feed production. The property is currently the Beacon Bay Marina. (Courtesy Frontenac Historical Society.)

American Malting Company malt house, c. 1900. This view is from the canal, with several packet boats moored at the dock. As is the norm for much of this county, the manufacturing is now gone and the economy is adjusting to tourism as its primary industry. In addition to the marina, this site also presently houses the Cayuga Wooden Boat Works, an antique boat restoration company.

Another view of the malt house, c. 1900. This view was taken from the railroad lines running through Cayuga. Cayuga Lake is located just to the other side of these buildings.

New York Central & Hudson River Railroad Station and water tank. The Mansfield House is the building on the far left. This photograph was taken from the foot of where the Cayuga Bridge once stood.

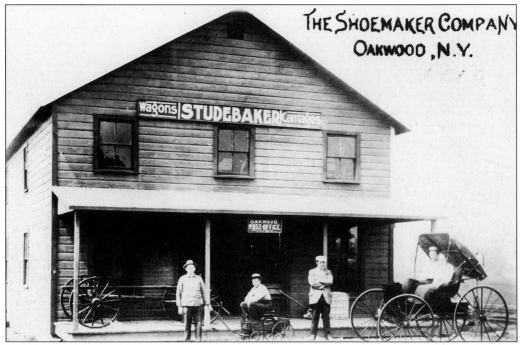

Post office and general store in Oakwood, 1910. Oakwood was once a busy railroad stop that included one of the largest ice houses in the area. This community was located about half way between Half Acre and Union Springs. Most of the village buildings are now gone. (Courtesy Frontenac Historical Society.)

The Spring Mill, Union Springs. This mill was built by George Howland in 1836. Flour was shipped from this location in 60-gallon oak casks made in Union Springs. Mill Street, which no longer exists, ran along the south side of the mill pond. The stone building eventually became part of a TRW plant, which also closed its doors. The stone for the mill building was quarried in Union Springs. (Courtesy Frontenac Historical Society.)

South Spring Pond on Factory Street, Union Springs, late nineteenth or early twentieth century. The central building was a cheese factory, the tall building on the left was the boiler to supply heat to the cheese factory, and the building on the right was the jelly factory, where it is said that "Certo" was invented by Milan F. Pratt. Cayuga Lake can be seen in the background. (Courtesy Frontenac Historical Society.)

Pavilion located on the southern end of Union Springs, late nineteenth or early twentieth century. Notice the unusual carousel chair ride on the right. One of the many steamers that transported passengers around the lake can be seen in the background.

Harbor, Union Springs, N. Y. on Cayuga Lake.

Union Springs Harbor. This view shows the white storehouse with docked ferry boats owned by Beardsley and Eldredge. In the background are McDonald's Point (also known as Pratts Point) and Springport Cove. (Courtesy Frontenac Historical Society.)

Steamer *Frontenac* and Frontenac Island, off shore of Union Springs on Cayuga Lake. The only island in all of the Finger Lakes, it is now a park owned by the village. The island was the site of many Native American burials, most of which were excavated and removed. (Courtesy Frontenac Historical Society.)

Remains of the *Frontenac*. This boat burned and sank in 1907 at Dill's Cove, a few miles south of Union Springs. It was enroute to the north from Ithaca at the time of the fire, and was carrying about fifty passengers.

Cayuga Street, Union Springs, late nineteenth century. This photograph shows the view looking south from the corner of Park Street. Most yards at this time were surrounded by fences to keep wandering livestock out. (Courtesy Frontenac Historical Society.)

West side of Cayuga Street, Union Springs, 1870s. Most of these buildings still stand today, with very few changes to their facades. Except for the types of vehicles and the unpaved road, this is generally how this business district looks today. (Courtesy Frontenac Historical Society.)

The Backus Estate, Union Springs, late nineteenth century. This is a view of the mansion, carriage house, and servants' quarters. Gillespie Chevrolet/Geo now stands on the site just to the front of the house. The house's foundation can still be seen behind the auto dealership. The street along the side, Madison Avenue, is still in use as an unpaved lane. The two carriage houses and part of the servants' quarters still stand. This estate stood in the center of the village, just across the street from the business district. (Courtesy Frontenac Historical Society.)

Old Sanitarium, Union Springs, late nineteenth or early twentieth century. This building, which served as the home of many businesses, stood where the present convenience store is located, on the corner of Cayuga and Park Streets. The structure was first built to be the Howland School. It later became a renowned sanitarium run by Dr. Franklin Pierce, and then the Grand Union Hotel. It was called the College Inn when Edward Glynn owned it. The last tenant was the American Legion, who occupied the north side while the rest of the building stood empty. It was demolished in the 1966. (Courtesy Frontenac Historical Society.)

Mosher's Quarry, nineteenth century. This quarry was located just east of the Union Springs village line on Center Street. Limestone quarrying was a major industry in the area, and many of the local homes and industries, such as the Spring Mill, were built using this stone. (Courtesy Frontenac Historical Society.)

Another view of Mosher's Quarry. Notice the lack of any heavy machinery. At the time of this photograph, most of the quarry work was done by hand. (Courtesy Frontenac Historical Society.)

Interior of a Union Springs blacksmith shop, nineteenth century. The Austin brothers, Charles and Coral, operated this blacksmith shop on Chapel Street in the area that is now the Trinity Church parking lot. (Courtesy Frontenac Historical Society.)

Young Monument, c. 1948. This unique self-styled monument near Great Gully was erected by Ernest J. and Margaret Swayze Young in memory of the Iroquois people and early European settlers whose home was the Upper Cayuga village site. The monument includes items that were excavated from the sites in the area.

George Carr's totem tree, Barber's Corners, early twentieth century. This unusual piece of folk art was carved by George Carr, a Civil War veteran and sometimes artist, poet, and coronet player. Carr began carving his tree in 1911, and included, among his intriguing combination of forty figures, an American eagle, a lion, a griffin, an idol holding a death skull, a criminal's head, and a teddy bear. The tree became a popular tourist stop, and Carr kept a registry of people who came to see his creation. He sold postcards of it, created a booklet, and eventually decorated the rest of his yard with equally unusual figures. Unfortunately, although his house remains, the totem tree has long since disappeared.

Four
Aurora and Vicinity

Aurora Dock, late nineteenth century. This is a great illustration of what were once the main modes of transportation in Cayuga County—railroads and boats. This view includes the paddlewheeler *T.D. Wilcox* at the Aurora Dock on Cayuga Lake. (Courtesy Louis J. Long Library, Wells College Archives.)

View of Aurora, looking up from the Aurora Dock, late nineteenth century. The picturesque village of Aurora is located just north of Long Point on the east side of Cayuga Lake. Wells College is located in Aurora, as are many historic homes. (Courtesy Louis J. Long Library, Wells College Archives.)

Way-Side Inn, showing Main Street, Aurora, N. Y

His is where I took dinner today. Delbert

Main Street, Aurora, early twentieth century. This view of Main Street includes the Way-Side Inn, founded in 1833 and now known as the Aurora Inn. It exists today much as it does in this photograph. The interior of the inn includes murals of the village of Aurora painted on the walls of the central hall. With rooms to let and a dining room that overlooks the lake, the inn is a popular place to visit. (Courtesy Ed Kabelac.)

Main Street, Aurora, late nineteenth century. Way-Side Inn and Morgan's Store are shown, with a Morgan's delivery wagon ready to take goods to customers. Morgan's Store, founded by Christopher Morgan in 1801, was a local landmark until it burned in 1919. (Courtesy Ed Kabelac.)

First National Bank, Aurora, early twentieth century. Emily Howland was voted to the board of directors of this bank, and she became one of the first women to be a bank director in America. This bank is still doing business as the Cayuga Lake National Bank, with the historic fabric of the structure respected and preserved. The window screens on the building are painted with landscape scenes; it is worth a visit just to see these unusual examples of American art. (Courtesy Ed Kabelac.)

Scipio Lodge 110, Aurora, 1955. This Masonic Lodge was constructed by the local chapter of the Royal Arch Masons in 1819–20. The cornerstone was laid by Governor DeWitt Clinton of New York. Its members included H.A. Morgan, S. Sherwood, and General Ledyard. Because of his father's membership in the organization, Lewis H. Morgan was allowed to use the building as a meeting place for his club, Order of the Iroquois. Lewis Morgan is known as the "father of anthropology" in America. The building includes an unusual inner-room design, featuring representations of significant symbols meaningful to the Masons. (Courtesy Ed Kabelac.)

Main Street, Aurora, early twentieth century. This is a view of the Armistead Co. Plumbing and Steam Fitting shop, and the Aurora Drug and Supply Co. (Courtesy Ed Kabelac.)

Lehigh Valley Railroad, near Aurora, early twentieth century. This view of the track along Cayuga Lake, looking to the north, shows the Wells College boathouse in the distance. This small cove is a popular site for Canada geese, who migrate along Cayuga Lake on their way to the Chesapeake Bay.

Wells College boathouse on Cayuga Lake, Aurora, early twentieth century. The two boys playing on the railroad tracks seem oblivious to the unusually high waves crashing upon the shore. This boathouse is currently still in use by the students of the college. (Courtesy Ed Kabelac.)

Cayuga Lake Military Academy cadets in formation outside the academy, late nineteenth century. Originally the Cayuga Academy boarding school, in the 1840s this institution had among its pupils Ely Parker, a Seneca Native American who became the aide-de-camp to General Grant, and later, the commissioner of Indian affairs under President Grant. In 1882, it became the Cayuga Lake Military Academy. Although the military academy left in 1898, the building continued to be used as a school until it burned in 1945. (Courtesy Ed Kabelac.)

Cadets of Cayuga Lake Military Academy, Aurora, 1882–98. The cadets are posed at the Presbyterian church. (Courtesy Ed Kabelac.)

Cayuga Lake Military Academy, late nineteenth century. The cadets are lined up in front of the Taylor House. The Taylor House is now used as the home of the president of Wells College. (Courtesy Louis J. Long Library, Wells College Archives.)

Original Old Main, Wells College, 1870s–1880s. This imposing structure was built in 1866 and stood on the Wells campus until it burned in 1888. (Courtesy Louis J. Long Library, Wells College Archives.)

Old Main following the fire, 1888. As this photograph shows, the building burned to the ground. (Courtesy Louis J. Long Library, Wells College Archives.)

Students participating in an unidentified event, Wells College, early twentieth century. Henry Wells' friend, Ezra Cornell, wanted Wells to locate his college in Ithaca but Wells insisted on maintaining it in Aurora. (Courtesy Louis J. Long Library, Wells College Archives.)

Glen Park, house of Henry Wells, Wells College, late nineteenth century. This view of Wells' 1852 house, looking toward Cayuga Lake, includes the foot bridge leading to the Wells College campus to the south. (Courtesy Louis J. Long Library, Wells College Archives.)

Aurora Medicinal and Sulfur Springs, near Aurora, 1920. Plant No. 1 produced 10,000 gallons of water a day. (Courtesy Louis J. Long Library, Wells College Archives.)

Retracing Sullivan's Trail, 1923. This photograph was taken by Charles R. Hunt at the site of the foundation of Roswell Franklin's house in Aurora. Franklin was the first white settler in Cayuga County. Defrauded of his land, he eventually took his own life. A log cabin once again sits on this site. Hunt was retracing the route of the Sullivan Campaign from Townersville, Pennsylvania, through Ithaca, New York. Of course, the campaign preceded Franklin's settling at this site, but his home was significant to the campaign because he was one of Sullivan's men.

Filling Station, Ledyard,1930s–1940s. This station serviced customers traveling along Route 34B. Ledyard is the first settlement north of King Ferry. (Courtesy Ed Kabelac.)

Mosher's Store and Poplar Ridge Post Office, Poplar Ridge, early twentieth century. Poplar Ridge, also on Route 34B, is located just to the east of Aurora and north of Ledyard. Route 34B features a number of small villages that have been able to maintain much of their nineteenth-century charm. (Courtesy Ed Kabelac.)

Eliza Mosher homestead on Brit Road, near Aurora, July 1938. Dr. Mosher, a pioneer for women entering the medical profession, was aided in her studies by Emily Howland of Sherwood, who was a leader in the Women's Rights Movement. This home is now all but gone. (Courtesy Ed Kabelac.)

Sherwood Select School, late nineteenth or early twentieth century. Built with funds from Emily Howland, this school was located in Sherwood, just to the east of Aurora. Ms. Howland's home is still standing just to the north of where this school was located. Although the school is gone, its bell is on display in the village.

Five
Southern Cayuga County: Genoa

Lehigh Valley Railroad, early twentieth century. Railroad tracks ran along the eastern side of Cayuga Lake at King Ferry. King Ferry was both a stop for the train and the eastern dock for a steam ferry that crossed the lake. This rail line, originally part of the old Cayuga Lake Railroad, was abandoned in 1951. The rail bed now serves as a lane to dozens of summer cottages along the lake. (Unless otherwise noted, all photographs in this chapter, including this one, are courtesy the Genoa Historical Association.)

Genoa Mill Dam, village of Genoa, early twentieth century. This dam was built in the early 1800s and abandoned in the 1930s, after being rebuilt several times following floods. It was in the stream between Smith's IGA and the Genoa Firehouse. Genoa is located in the Salmon Creek Valley between Cayuga and Owasco Lakes, near the southern end of the county.

Genoa Roller Mill, village of Genoa, nineteenth century. The water to power the mill was supplied by the Genoa Mill Dam. At one point, there were two gristmills located on Salmon Creek. This mill was located on the east side of the creek, where the Genoa Firehouse now stands.

Creamery, village of Genoa, early twentieth century. This creamery, built in the mid-nineteenth century, was located on the west side of Salmon Creek, south of Route 90.

Plowing the field, early twentieth century. Women worked the land too! This hard-working lady, posing proudly with her team of horses, was local Genoa resident Frances Marshall Nedrow's mother.

T.C. McCormick Machinery Dealership, village of King Ferry, 1912. Farmers gathered at the local dealership in the spring with their mules, horses, and excited family members to draw home their new farm equipment. The character of the town of Genoa has always been that of a rural, agricultural community.

Jump hay-pressers Pete Cummings and Joe Dempsey (center), 1905. They are on the press that was located between King Ferry and Genoa. The land between the lakes offered such prime dairy farming that even after the Midwest opened to settlement, these farms remained active.

George Curtis and family, near Five Corners, c. 1915. The whole family proudly poses for a picture in front of their newly erected barn, which replaced one lost to fire.

Driscoll's Flax Oil Mill at Little Salmon Creek, nineteenth century. One hundred acres of flax were grown just east of this mill. A millstone from this place is located on the premises of the Rural Museum in King Ferry.

Atwater Saw Mill, King Ferry, early twentieth century. This building was located east of the current King Ferry Bowling Alley and Pizzeria of 1996.

F.T. Atwater General Store, southwest corner in King Ferry. This store was demolished in the 1920s and replaced by a Ford dealership and garage.

Kendall House, early twentieth century. This longtime landmark in King Ferry, now known as the King Ferry Hotel, is actually the second hotel and tavern on this spot. The first, built in 1814, burned in 1844. Today, the King Ferry Hotel is a popular eating establishment that has been restored to look much as it does in this photograph.

King Ferry looking south, intersection of Routes 90 and 34B, 1930s. This view from the grounds of the King Ferry Hotel includes the Ford dealership, with its unusual land-locked lighthouse, built on the site of F.T. Atwater's General Store. For a time, the dealership was the site of a

canoe-building company. Unfortunately, the lighthouse was removed when Route 34B was widened. The country store on the left still serves the village.

Foot of West Hill in Genoa, looking toward King Ferry. This dirt road is now Route 90, which runs from Homer to Montezuma. Today, the Route 90 Association promotes a 50-mile garage sale that takes place yearly on the last weekend in July.

Main Street's former business block, north of Route 90 in Genoa. This block was gradually abandoned after World War II, and then demolished in the 1980s.

An elegant Queen Anne home of the early twentieth century. This structure is located at the foot of West Hill, south side of Route 90 in Genoa.

Genoa residential street, north off Route 90, early 1900s. Note the style and detail in the porches visible on these houses. Porches often provided a lovely view for residents and an invitation to visitors.

George Morrison residence, north of Five Corners. Abandoned as a home in the 1930s, all that remains of this farmstead is the rich land on which it was built.

"The Rugmaker" at his loom at the Forks of Creek, late nineteenth or early twentieth century. Housewives from the area saved rags from worn-out fabrics and took them to "recycle" as throw rugs.

Genoa Citizen's Band, early twentieth century. This musical ensemble later became the Southern Cayuga Band.

Genoa fair grand stand, early twentieth century. This annual fair drew large crowds for over a quarter century.

Celebration of the Auburn-Ithaca "Short Line Railroad," Genoa, 1908. This railroad succeeded a branch of the "Midland," which ran from 1869 to 1891. Remnants of the railroad bed can still be seen paralleling Route 34. Many of the small stations are also still standing in the villages that the line traveled through.

"Motor car, the latest thing in railroad equipment, Now in use on the 'short line' between Auburn and Ithaca NY." The Short Line Railroad was in operation briefly, from the early 1900s until 1923, and connected Auburn and Ithaca via Mapleton, Venice, Genoa, and Lansing. Although eagerly anticipated when it opened, the Short Line proved unable to compete with the advent of the automobile. (Postcard from the collection of the Cayuga Museum.)

The *Busy Bee*. This ferryboat operated on Cayuga Lake between King Ferry and Kidders during the nineteenth and twentieth centuries. George Westinghouse and Captain James Quick (at right) are shown in the insert. Today, there is a growing interest in reviving a modern-day ferryboat service between the centers of Cayuga and Seneca Counties, for both passengers and automobiles.

Early touring car, *c.* 1910. Take note of the acetylene lights. Dr. James W. Skinner (driver) and family pose for the picture in front of the Genoa Hospital, which he built in 1916. The building was destroyed by fire in January 1954.

Samuel Dexter Fessenden with his first tractor on the family farm, late 1920s. This farm in King Ferry has been in the same family since 1863, and it is still contributing today to the important agricultural economy of the county. The tractor, though, has long since been put out to pasture.

Little Giants Baseball Team, c. 1940. This local team, which played ball from 1928 until 1942, is shown here at the ball park in King Ferry, west of Our Lady of the Lake Catholic Church.

Six

Weedsport and
Port Byron

New York and West Shore Depot, Weedsport, late nineteenth or early twentieth century. Weedsport was a primary crossroads for Auburn and the rest of Cayuga County because of its location on the Erie Canal and the rail lines between Syracuse and Rochester, as well as Auburn north to Fair Haven. (Unless otherwise noted, the photographs in this chapter are courtesy the Lock 52 Historical Society of Port Byron.)

The National Hotel in Port Byron, originally under the proprietorship and management of E.B. Buck. Later, William H. Galt became the proprietor. Formerly known as the Park Hotel (among other names), it is now the Rock and Rye Tavern. The water for the 1883 fountain in front of the hotel was provided by the Howard House, located on Utica Street. Rush Howard was paid $5 per year for maintaining the fountain, which was taken down when Route 31 was enlarged.

View of the Masonic block, Main Street, Port Byron. The Masonic building, constructed just prior to the Civil War, is located on the corner of Main and Church Streets. The first floor was rented to businesses, including Blake's Pharmacy, which was located in the left-hand corner. The lodge rooms were on the second floor. The third floor, which is said to be suspended from the rafters, was used for dances and as a theater.

Bird's-eye view of Port Byron. This photograph was taken from the Mount Pleasant Cemetery area looking northwest. The trolley tracks to Auburn can be seen in the foreground beside the road going to Auburn. The tallest building is the old I.R. Waren flour mill. The mill pond and the raceway to the mill are in the center of the picture.

West side of South Main Street, Port Byron, late nineteenth century. From left to right are: the Dayharsh building, a hardware store that became the home of the H.C. Gutchess mincemeat factory, the first firehouse (with the bell on the tower), and the post office and *Port Byron Chronicle* offices (in the last building).

A view of Pine Street looking west. The trolley can be seen at the foot of Pine Street. The building of the Lock 52 Historical Society of Port Byron is located on the right side near the end of the street. From this angle, only a window can be seen of the house.

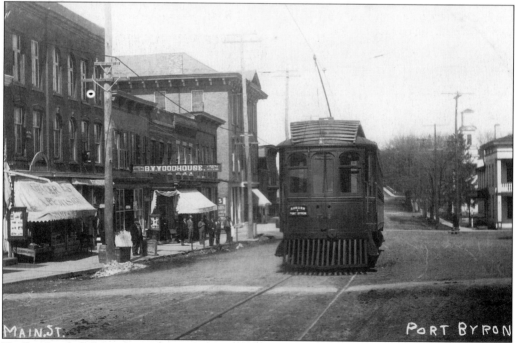

Trolley headed for Auburn. This trolley is on the Auburn and Northern Trolley tracks that went down the middle of Main Street. These tracks connected to the Rochester, Syracuse, and Eastern Trolley tracks by a "Y" in front of the R. S. & E. station. The R.S. & E. existed between 1906 and 1931. The trolley station is now the American Legion building.

The December 24, 1935 fire at Port Byron High School. Fortunately, the school was closed for Christmas vacation—otherwise many lives would have been lost. The interior was constructed of wood which had dried out over the years, making it an easy victim to fire. A third building was erected on this site and was in use until a new high school building was added to the A.A. Gates Elementary School and the Middle School on Maple Avenue. Apartments are in the old high school building on Church Street.

Kittie Rhodes, a native of Port Byron, was a successful actress who later formed her own repertory company which performed all over the United States. Ms. Rhodes brought her company to Auburn each year, and also held some performances in Port Byron. Following her retirement, she lived at Hayden's Mill south of Auburn until her marriage to second husband, Louis Henderson, after which they moved to Newburgh, NY. Kittie Rhodes died in Newburgh in 1937, but was brought back to Port Byron and buried in Mount Pleasant Cemetery.

View of the aqueduct over the Owasco Outlet and the dam near Wilt's Mill. The supports of the aqueduct are columns constructed of local stone. The sides of this aqueduct were made of wood, and only a portion of the stone remains today.

A closer look at the dam and a part of Wilt's Mill on the Owasco Outlet. Note that the dam is made of wooden timbers.

View of the old aqueduct over the Owasco Outlet on the original route of the Erie canal, before it was widened, through the village of Port Byron. The large white building on the left is St. John's Catholic Church.

The west end of Lock 52, to the west end of Port Byron, on the Erie Canal. The lock was a double lock allowing two boats to go through at the same time, even if they were traveling in opposite directions. The lock tender's house is situated between the two locks. There were always two men for the shifts at the locks. Frank Emmons, Mattie Rooker, Wash Dinehart, and Nate Elliot were a few of Port Byron's lock tenders. This site is presently being developed into a canal heritage site.

Boat headed east out of the lock. The water is high in the lock because the water level on the east was higher than on the west. It is also clear which direction the boat was traveling because the bow of the boat is curved, whereas the stern is flat.

Caldwell's Coal Yard, on the south side of the canal. The barges are going under the Utica Street bridge. The hill in the background is a drumlin, created by the last glaciers that moved through this region. Drumlins are unusual glacial features only found in a few sites south of the Great Lakes.

Boat in the west end of the lock. This vessel is waiting to be locked up so it can proceed east (the low water level indicates it is in the west end of the lock). Upon touring this lock, be certain to look for the rope grooves cut into the limestone at the lock's ends, created through many years of boats being pulled through the lock.

O.B. & Hull Tanner Dry Dock, Port Byron, late nineteenth or early twentieth century. The Tanner Dry Dock was the largest drydock on the Erie Canal. The Tanners built and repaired all types of boats. A large canal barge under construction can be seen in the background. Two of the men in the picture are Byron France, a Tanner employee, and Sherman Tanner, a Long Island businessman. The third figure is unknown. This drydock is part of a newly developed park that also includes Lock 52, an inn, a mule barn, and other features unique to life on the Erie Canal. A museum also proposed at the site which will be housed in the power station for the electric trolleys, showing the changing modes of travel that evolved at this site.

View of the Tanner Dry Dock, looking east, showing boats tied up on the canal and boats under construction. This picture was taken at the time that steamboats plied the Erie Canal. The drydock was on the south side of the Erie Canal. The boat in front of the building by the tree is ready to be launched.

The *Floretta*, tied up at the Tanner Dry Dock. Many boats, including the steamers *Mohawk*, *Queen*, *Nautilus*, and *Iroquois*, came on a yearly basis. A ledger showed that the Tanner Dry Dock serviced as many as three hundred boats and charged from $2 to $4 for boat storage. The fee depended on the size of the boat.

A closer view of boats under construction at the Tanner Dry Dock. The raceway that controlled the water level in the drydock is visible in the middle of the picture. Tugs, scows, and lakers were repaired at Tanner's facility. These boats were able to enter Cayuga Lake through the Cayuga-Seneca Canal, which intersected the Erie Canal at Montezuma.

The Tanner Dry Dock, late nineteenth or early twentieth century. The last boat to be built at the Tanner Dry Dock was built by Leon France and delivered to a Brooklyn longshoreman. Potatoes were used for ballast to keep the boat low enough to go under the bridge. The captain bought the potatoes for 50¢ a bushel and hoped to sell them for the same price in New York City. In the time it took the men to deliver the boat, the potatoes had gone up to $4 a bushel, paying for the cost of the boat's hull.

Seven

Heading North: Conquest and Cato

Lehigh Valley Railroad Station, Cato, twentieth century. This crowd of Sunday school picnickers is anxiously waiting to board the train to Fair Haven for the annual Sunday school picnic. (Courtesy Civic Heritage Historical Society.)

Village Blacksmith, Conquest, c. 1900. This postcard was produced for sale at Van Aukin's General Store in the village of Conquest. Conquest is a small community located in the north-central region of the county. (Courtesy Eleanor Aldrich Collection.)

Maple Street, Conquest, c. 1900. This photograph looks east toward what is now Slayton Road. The hotel and post office are now the site of the Conquest Fire Department. (Courtesy Eleanor Aldrich Collection.)

Seneca River and Barge Canal at Mosquito Point, c. 1900. This postcard was also produced for sale at Van Aukin's General Store. (Courtesy Eleanor Aldrich Collection.)

Members of the Conquest Grange, c. 1935–1940. Just what is everyone looking at?

Main Street, Spring Lake, early 1900s. Judson Green was the owner of the general store, which also served as the post office. Through the economic changes of the last century, Spring Lake has shrunk in size and many of the homes and businesses are now gone. It is a community that is located well off the beaten path, in a very rural portion of the county west of Conquest. (Courtesy Eleanor Aldrich Collection.)

Spring Lake, house next to general store, c. 1900. This house still stands but the porch roof has fallen, the paint is long gone, and the structure's future is very uncertain. (Courtesy Eleanor Aldrich Collection.)

Spring Lake Methodist Church, early twentieth century. The Spring Lake Methodist Church was built in 1859 by Nathan Swift. It merged with Conquest church in 1970 to form the Countryside United Methodist Church.

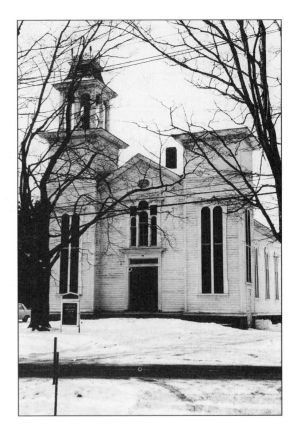

Hotel in Spring Lake, early 1900s. (Courtesy Eleanor Aldrich Collection.)

Cobblestone house on West Main Street, Cato, *c.* 1900. Once the residence of Major John Savery, who was wounded in the Civil War, it is now an apartment house and a well-known local historic landmark.

Business district, Cato, *c.* 1900. Although the brick block was replaced by a gas station, the two wood-framed buildings remain as the oldest commercial structures in Cato. This site is now the intersection of Routes 34 and 370. (Courtesy Civic Heritage Historical Society.)

Hapman & Goodfellow Coal Yard, Cato, c. 1900. This establishment was located next to the Lehigh Valley Railroad line. The building is long gone, demolished not by urban renewal but by a runaway truck. (Courtesy Civic Heritage Historical Society.)

Dairymen's League Plant, Cato, 1941. A diner now rests at this spot on Route 34, and dairying has ended for many area farmers. Note that the roadway is constructed of concrete rather than asphalt. Original concrete lies beneath many of the roads in central New York; it exposes its presence every now and then by causing the present pavement to crack where it overlaps the shoulder. (Courtesy Civic Heritage Historical Society.)

Main Street, Cato, c. 1900. This view of the northern side of the business district in Cato recalls its appearance before the fire of 1918. Note the popularity of awnings.

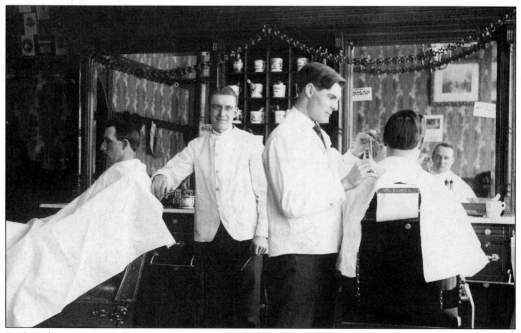

Barber shop, Cato, early twentieth century. At least one of these men is paying attention to the business at hand! Notice the individual shaving mugs on display and ready to use.

The members of the Emerson Church Conference, town of Conquest, c. 1900. The towns of Conquest and Victory were given their unique names after succeeding to win their independence. (Courtesy Eleanor Aldrich Collection.)

Ernest G. Tabor, posing with his stuffed bird collection, 1883. Tabor (1854–1964) was a clerk on the board of supervisors; a student of Iroquois history; a collector of coins, stamps, and Native American artifacts; and an amateur ornithologist and taxidermist. From this description, it seems fair to say that he was certainly a Renaissance man. (Courtesy Marion Dudley.)

Four Corners, Meridian, 1880. From left to right on Main Street are: the Palmeter Hotel, the Presbyterian church, A.M. West's grocery and drug store, and the bandstand.

The Morley House, Meridian, *c.* 1900. This Greek Revival structure was built by William Smith Ingham in 1835. It was the residence of J. Sprague Morley when this photograph was taken. (Courtesy Marion Dudley.)

Smith & Cornish Furniture & Undertaking, Meridian, 1926. In 1815, this building was the Ingham Store. Today it is the Colonial Inn, standing out as a distinctive local historic landmark. (Courtesy Marion Dudley.)

Meridian Presbyterian Church, c. 1900. Built in 1839, the church was sold to the Meridian Fire Department and used as a bingo hall in the 1970s. It was destroyed by fire on January 3, 1996, in the most recent of a long line of fires in this county.

Meridian Fire Department and hand pumper, Meridian, 1903. These dedicated individuals pose here with what was, at the time, the most modern firefighting equipment money could buy.

J.D. Bloomfield Grocery delivery wagon, late nineteenth or early twentieth century. One has to wonder why these men are wearing masks. (Courtesy Marion Dudley.)

Steamroller and crew, East Main Street, Meridian, 1920s. The house in the background was the home of David Rockwell, the builder of a local foundry in 1833. (Courtesy Marion Dudley.)

Main Street, Meridian. This view shows some early automobiles and riders, obviously enjoying festivities of some sort. (Courtesy Marion Dudley.)

Main Street, Meridian, 1920s. Getting ready for the evening of July 3, an annual tradition in Meridian. (Courtesy Marion Dudley.)

A lively game of croquet, early twentieth century. This game is being played on the lawn of the Lucas residence on Hollister Street in Meridian. The man of good fortune prepares to swing his mallet. (Courtesy Marion Dudley.)

Meridian Union School and pupils, early twentieth century. The building has long been used as a private residence. (Courtesy Marion Dudley.)

Lawrence Block, Meridian, early twentieth century. This reputed station on the Underground Railroad burned in 1909. (Courtesy Marion Dudley.)

John Judge Hotel, Meridian, early twentieth century. This building, also known at various times as Palmeter's, Acker's, and the Eagle Hotel, was built prior to 1840. It is now an apartment house. (Courtesy Marion Dudley.)

Merritt Hotel and grounds, early twentieth century. Also known as the Meridian House, this structure was built in 1893 on the site of a long line of local taverns. (Courtesy Marion Dudley.)

Bloomfield Hotel, also known as Bloomfield's Landing, early twentieth century, Cross Lake. This building stands today, with enlargements, and is now known as The Cross Lake Inn. Cross Lake is a shallow lake in a low land that today serves as part of the active Erie Canal. (Courtesy Marion Dudley.)

Meridian Baptist Church, Meridian, 1910. (Courtesy Marion Dudley.)

Bloomfield Block, Meridian, early twentieth century. This building once housed stores, a post office, and social rooms. The post office remains today in the right wing of the building. (Courtesy Marion Dudley.)

Eight

North, Near and Far: Victory, Ira, and Sterling

George Wiggin's store and home in Ira, *c.* 1900. The boys are Mort Graham (left) and Ralph "Pete" Hull (sitting on the wooden steps) in front of the store in Ira. The store and home of the Wiggins family burned in the early 1940s. (Courtesy Dorothy Southard.)

Customers lined up for service at James Fuller's Blacksmith Shop, Ira Hill, in the winter, *c.* 1910. (Courtesy Dorothy Southard.)

Town of Ira District #6 School, Ira, *c.* 1920s. This school burned in August of 1936 or 1937. The fire that destroyed it began in a house just west of the school. (Courtesy Carol Easton Reed and Dorothy Southard.)

Barefoot boys in front of the Ira Hotel, c. 1900. The boys are, from left to right: Mort Graham, Charley Johnson, Ralph "Pete" Hull, and John Wiggins. (Courtesy Dorothy Southard.)

Mrs. George Horrigan (Florence Goodrich) and her smiling son Ivan, town of Ira, c. 1900. Mrs. Horrigan was the school teacher in the District #6 School in Ira. (Courtesy Dorothy Southard.)

Truman Weller sitting on his steam engine, town of Ira, 1920s. Truman did custom threshing of grains for farmers in the local area. (Courtesy Robert Weller.)

The Lehigh Valley Railroad station at Ira Station, early 1920s. Operations on the line from the village of Cato north to Fair Haven ceased in 1953 for economic reasons. This area in the north-central region of the county has the same rich soil that is found in the southern end of the county, but the growing season is shorter, with the area receiving an appreciably greater amount of lake-effect snow than the area south of the Erie Canal. (Courtesy Dorothy Southard.)

Town of Ira Highway employees at the stone quarry between Lysander and Lloyd Roads, 1940. These work crews are preparing to fix the roads in the eastern side of the town. (Courtesy Dorothy Southard.)

Diggers in front of Bill Stahlnecker's property, early twentieth century. These men from the village of Victory are digging a sluiceway toward Red Creek from four corners in Victory. The county is primarily agricultural and its histories are mostly personal, about individual struggles within small communities. In the last hundred years, the population count has barely changed. (Courtesy Marian Houghtaling.)

Victory Mercantile, Victory, 1904–1905. Ed Hornburg and Roy Houghtaling were the owners of the Victory Mercantile, later known as the Smith and Dunbar Store. Customers could buy everything from oysters to phonograph machines at this general store. (Courtesy Marian Houghtaling.)

Workers in front of Stum's Mill, 1904. Stum's was a grain mill in the town of Victory. (Courtesy Marian Houghtaling.)

Business district, Victory, 1900. The Smith and Dunbar Store, complete with living quarters, is the light-colored structure on the left. Bacon's Egg Room is on the right. Oral French's home and movie house is in the center. (Courtesy Marian Houghtaling.)

The Grand Hotel once stood next to the present Grange Hall. On the top floor was the ballroom—the scene of many a gala event. (Courtesy Marion Haughtaling.)

Victory Post Office, early twentieth century. The old post office once stood next to the present firehouse. (Courtesy Marion Haughtaling.)

Hager Store, on the west side of the road in Victory. This building was later home to the Rock Garden Cheese factory, owned by Joseph Raiti. (Courtesy Marion Haughtaling.)

District #5 Victory Village School in 1926. The building is now Reverend and Beatrice Williams' house.

Victory Band, early twentieth century. They appear to be standing on the shore of Lake Ontario. (Courtesy Marion Haughtaling.)

Robinson & Phillips General Store, Main Street, Fair Haven,1880s. Notice the delivery wagon waiting by the building. Fair Haven was a port village on Lake Ontario that was settled at a natural harbor. It was an important port that at one time featured a gigantic coal trestle for loading ships from trains.

Crosswalk from hotel to post office, Fair Haven, early twentieth century. This view shows the M.E. Church, and the Griggs, Howell, and Phillips Blocks. (Courtesy Ray Sant Collection, Sterling Historical Society.)

Interior, unidentified Fair Haven soda fountain, 1910s. (Courtesy Ray Sant Collection, Sterling Historical Society.)

Lunch at the Allen Inn, Fair Haven, early twentieth century. The Allen Inn was built to handle the local railroad trade. (Courtesy Ray Sant Collection, Sterling Historical Society.)

Beach at Fair Haven, Lake Ontario, early twentieth century. The beach at Fair Haven is a now park that features swimming, fishing, boating camping, picnicking, and many other summer activities. (Courtesy Ray Sant Collection, Sterling Historical Society.)

Range Light, on the south end of the west pier, Fair Haven, late nineteenth or early twentieth century. (Courtesy Ray Sant Collection, Sterling Historical Society.)

Fowler-Wells Octagon House, Fair Haven, late nineteenth or early twentieth century. This house, also known as the Bacon Farm, is located on the western side of the bay. Lorenzo Fowler, brother of Orson Fowler (the creator of the Octagon house fad in America), built this house with his brother-in-law, Samuel Wells. Together they also owned a publishing company, with plants in both New York City and Auburn. This building was razed in 1954. (Courtesy Ray Sant Collection, Sterling Historical Society.)

Big Bluffs near Fair Haven, early twentieth century. The shore of Lake Ontario has both high bluffs and protected bays. Because of the size of the lake, the shores are always changing. (Courtesy Ray Sant Collection, Sterling Historical Society.)

First power ice saw in Fair Haven, pulled by Frank Eldredge, early twentieth century. Eldredge, a supervisor for the Lehigh Valley Railroad coal operations at North Fair Haven, was also the owner of Garrett Coal and Ice Company, the principal supplier of ice for the city of Auburn. (Courtesy Ray Sant Collection, Sterling Historical Society.)

Ice on an Eldredge conveyor belt, Fair Haven, early twentieth century. (Courtesy Ray Sant Collection, Sterling Historical Society.)

Loading ice on boxcars for shipment, Fair Haven, early twentieth century. (Courtesy Ray Sant Collection, Sterling Historical Society.)

Lehigh Valley R.R. tug *Cortland* at docks near rail yard, North Fair Haven, early twentieth century. This tug, earlier named the *K.T. Wilbur*, was operated by Captain T. McGuire. (Courtesy Ray Sant Collection, Sterling Historical Society.)

George H. Bunts on the *Snipe* at Downey Dock, Fair Haven, early twentieth century. Note the swastika on the boat's flag: it was a popular Native American design prior to the day that it was invested with other, very powerful meanings. (Courtesy Ray Sant Collection, Sterling Historical Society.)

Building on the breakwater, Fair Haven, late nineteenth or early twentieth century. (Courtesy Ray Sant Collection, Sterling Historical Society.)

Boardwalk and lighthouse, Fair Haven, early twentieth century. First lit in 1872, this structure guided ships until it was replaced by a metal-frame automatic light in 1943. Many people tend to forget that ocean-going vessels are able to dock in Cayuga County. (Courtesy Ray Sant Collection, Sterling Historical Society.)

The steamer *Arundel* at a coal trestle, Fair Haven, early twentieth century. The *Arundel* plied the waters of Lake Ontario, and made stops at Rochester, Oswego, and Thousand Islands.

Steamer loading at coal trestle, Fair Haven, early twentieth century, Fair Haven. Coal was the principal item of export at Fair Haven. This massive coal trestle, which operated until 1936, had the ability to hold sixteen full coal-cars. The trestle eventually burnt, a not-so-surprising event considering the explosive nature of coal dust.

Drying sails, coal trestle at Fair Haven, late nineteenth or early twentieth century. At one time, the big ships were a common sight at Fair Haven. (Courtesy Ray Sant Collection, Sterling Historical Society.)

Results of a carp fishing expedition, Sterling Center, early twentieth century. (Courtesy Ray Sant Collection, Sterling Historical Society.)

Sterling Center bridge, 1911. Sterling Center, located to the east of Fair Haven, is south of the bluffs on Lake Ontario and does not have a port. (Courtesy Ray Sant Collection, Sterling Historical Society.)

Harvesting apples at Crocketts, early twentieth century. (Courtesy Ray Sant Collection, Sterling Historical Society.)

Florence DeMount, 1967. She is standing in front of the post office in Sterling. (Courtesy Ray Sant Collection, Sterling Historical Society.)

View of Lake Ontario, Fair Haven, early twentieth century. The huge coal trestle can be seen in the background.

Lighthouse, Fair Haven, late nineteenth or early twentieth century. A past beacon to world commerce, it is situated on the northern edge of the county. (Courtesy Ray Sant Collection, Sterling Historical Society.)